We Love To Swear

Coloring Book

By

S.B. Nozaz

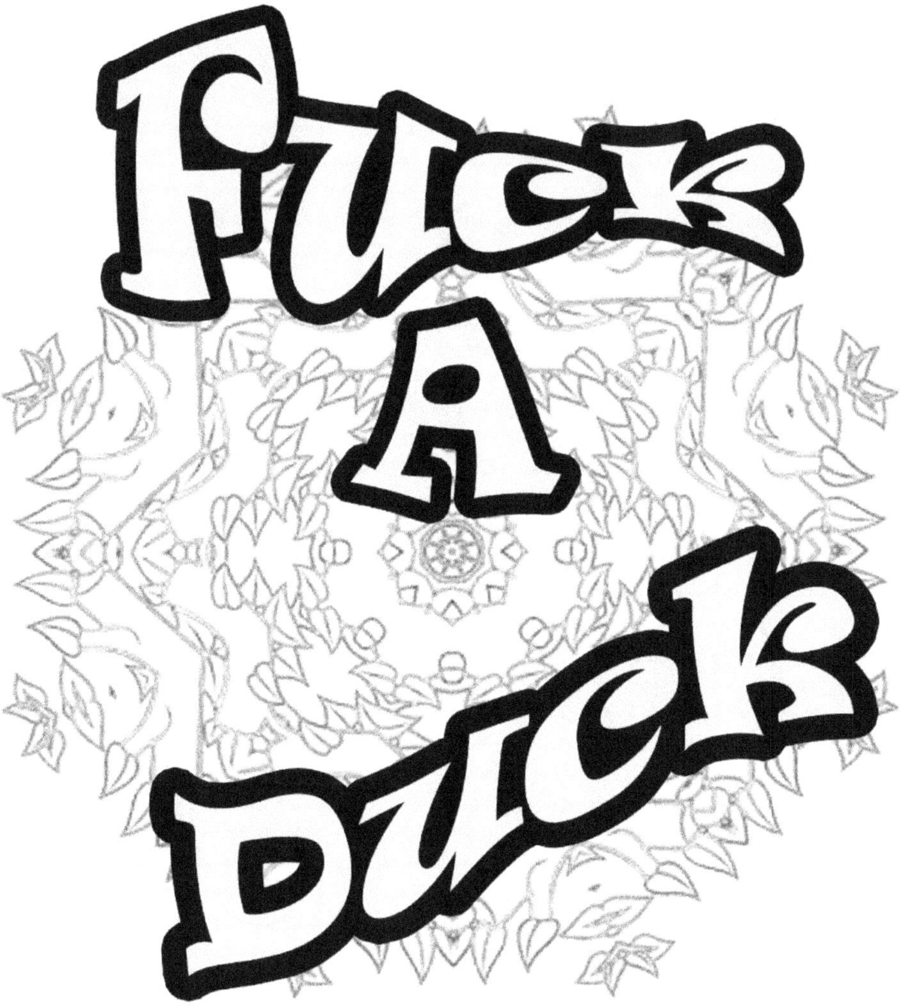
Fuck
A
Duck

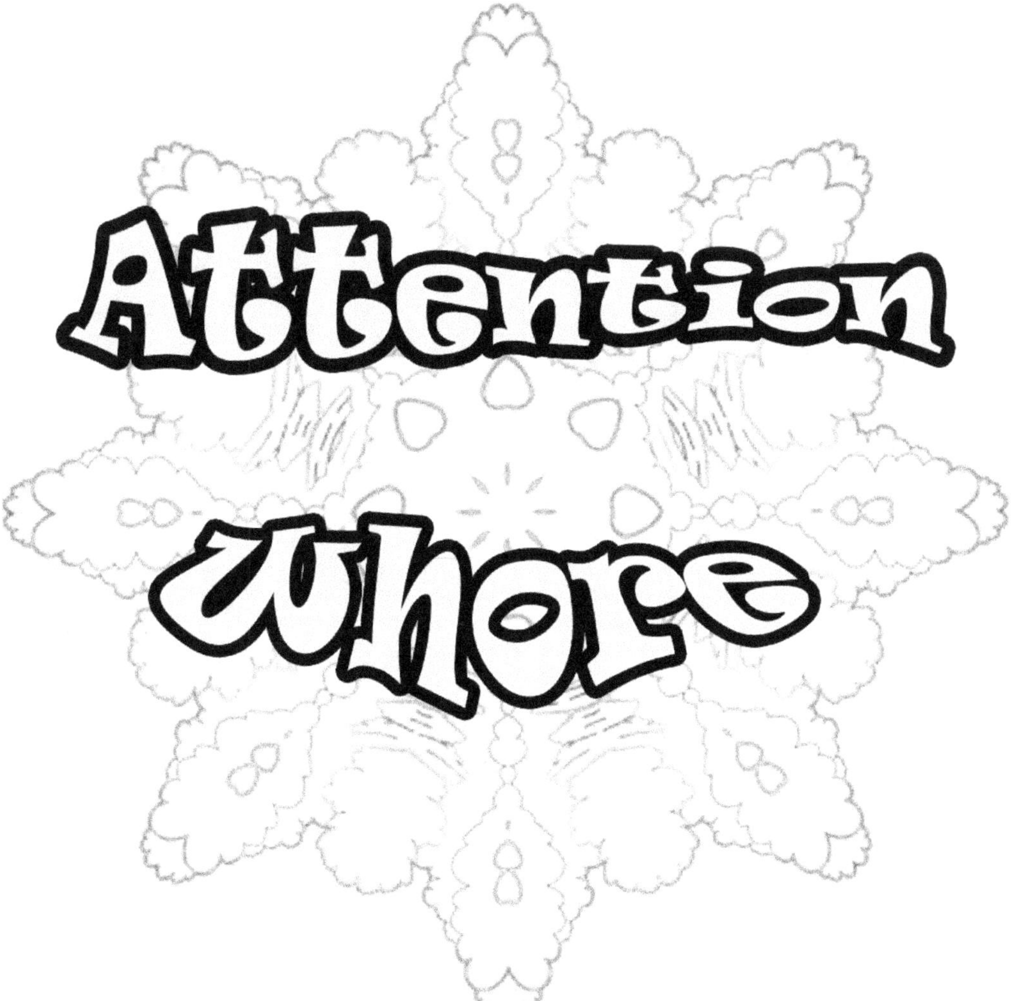
Attention
whore

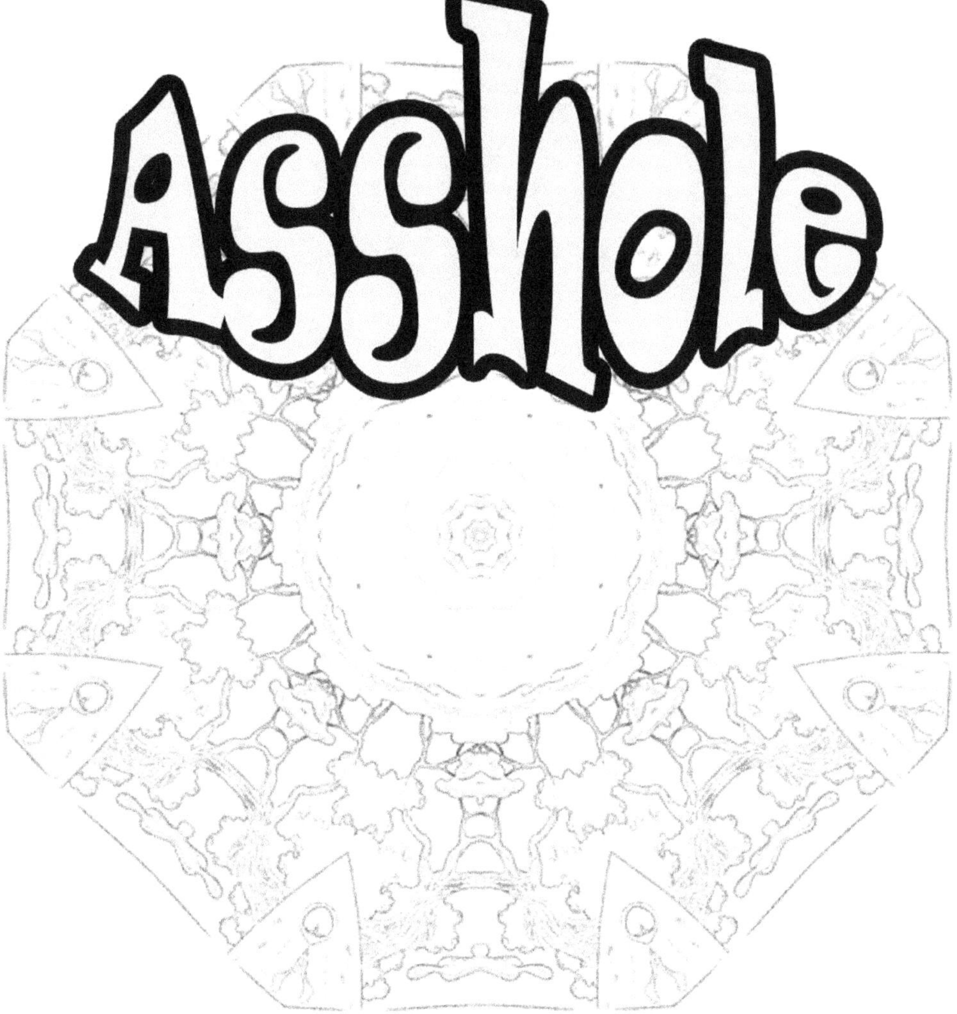
Asshole

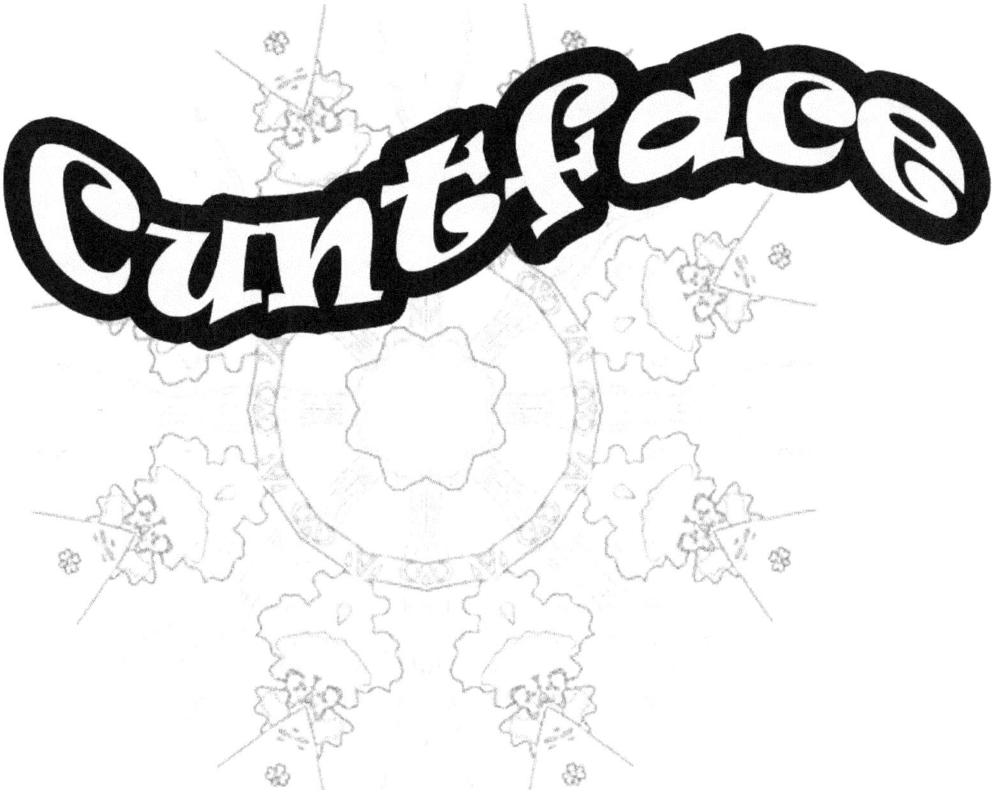
Cuntface

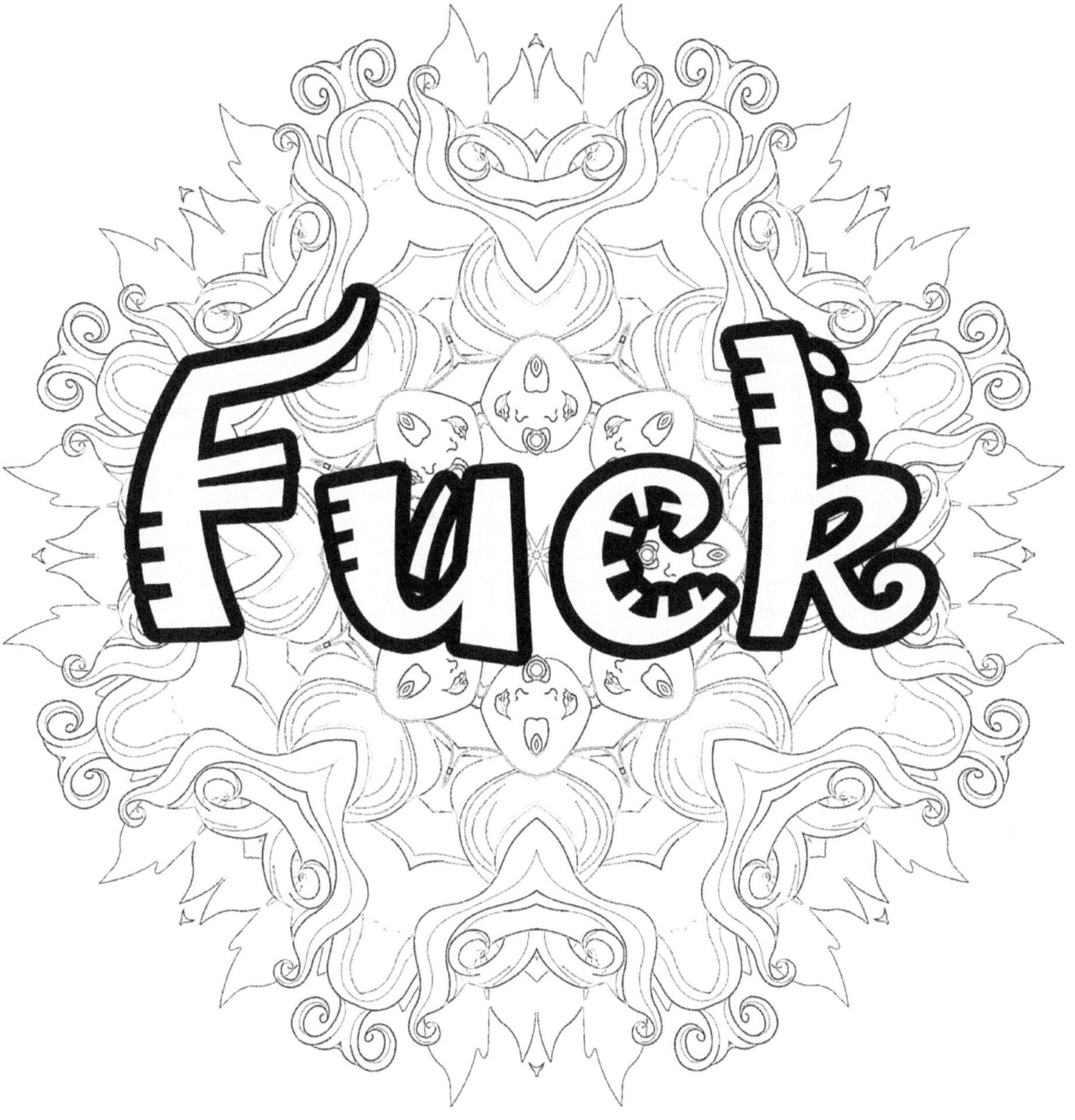
Fuck

Cock

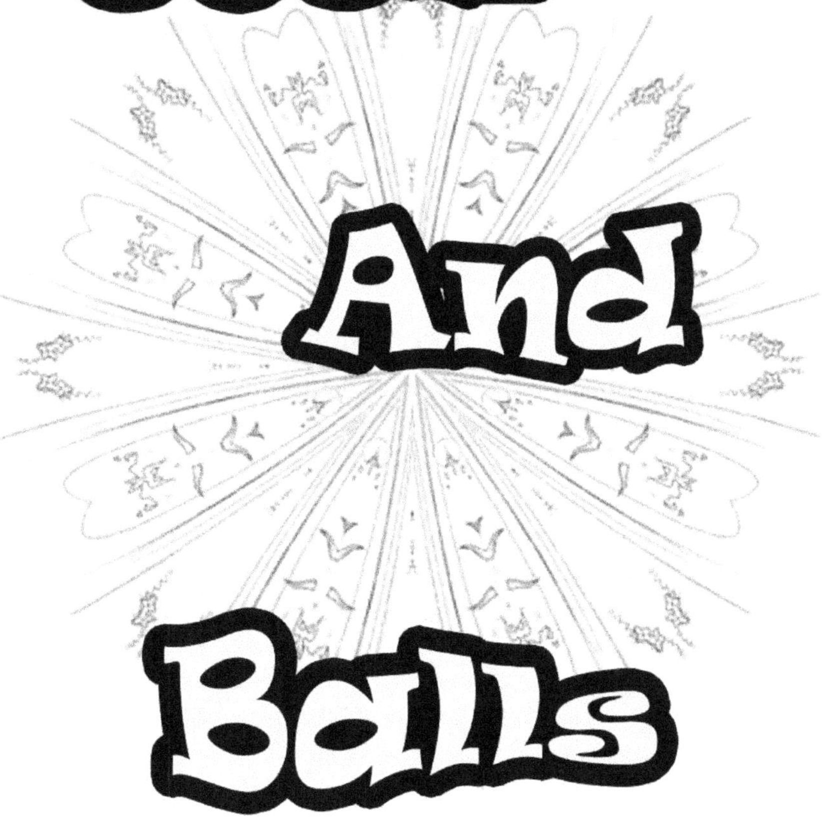

And

Balls

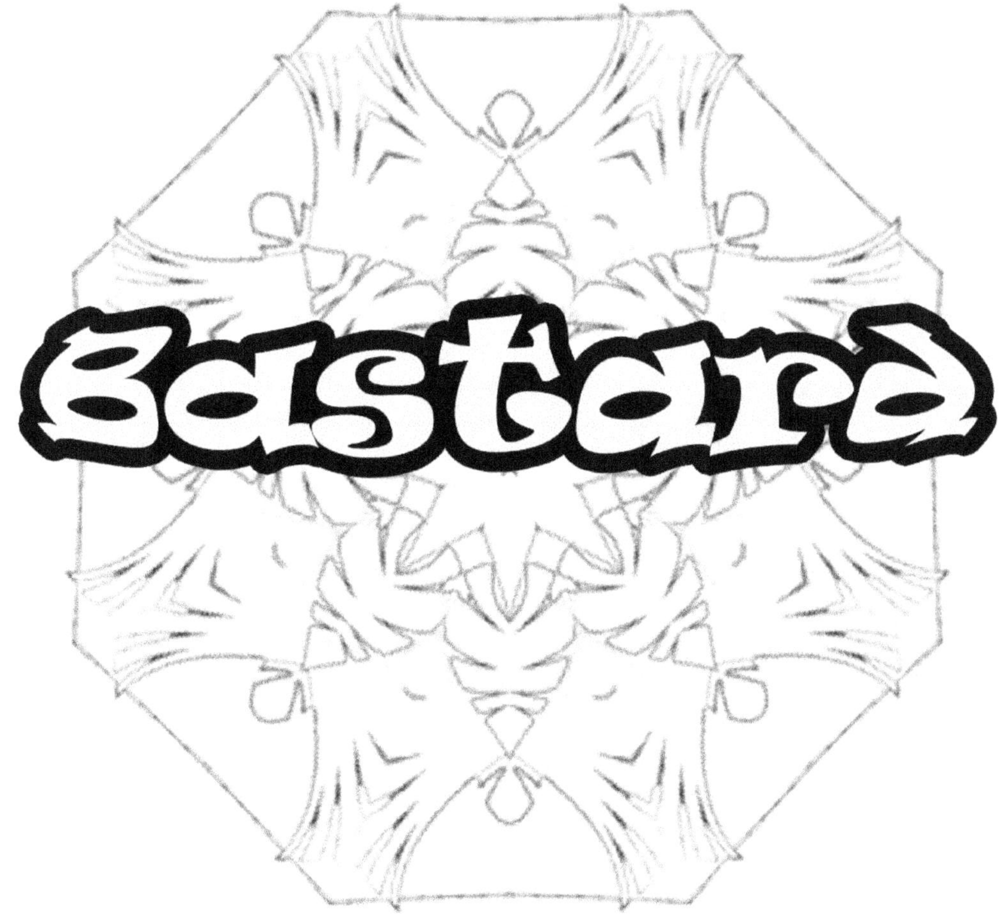
Bastard

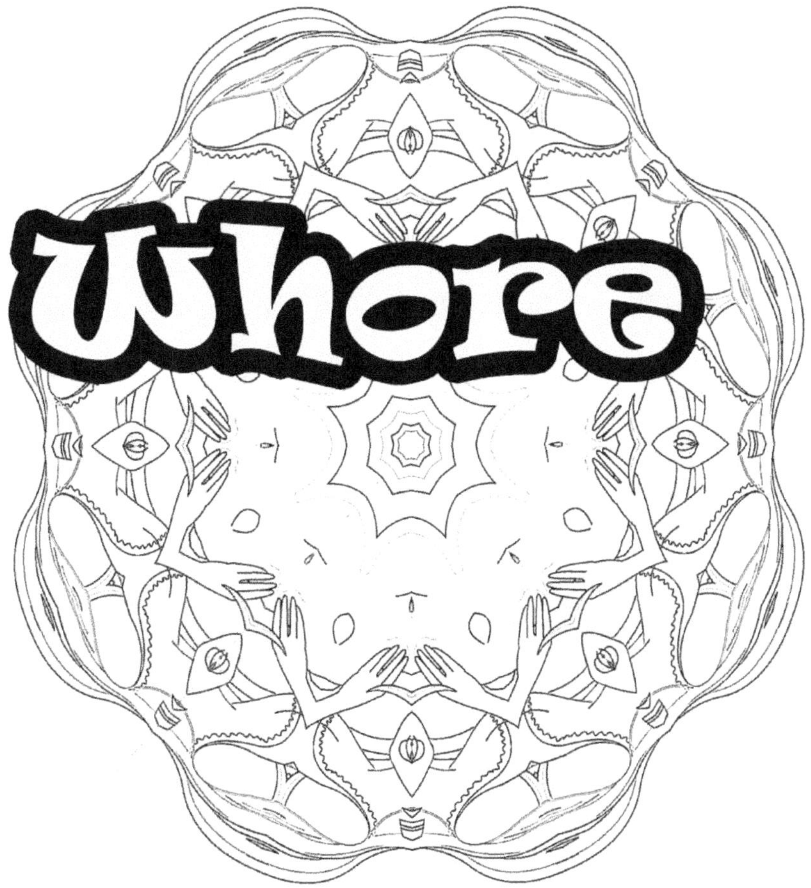
Whore

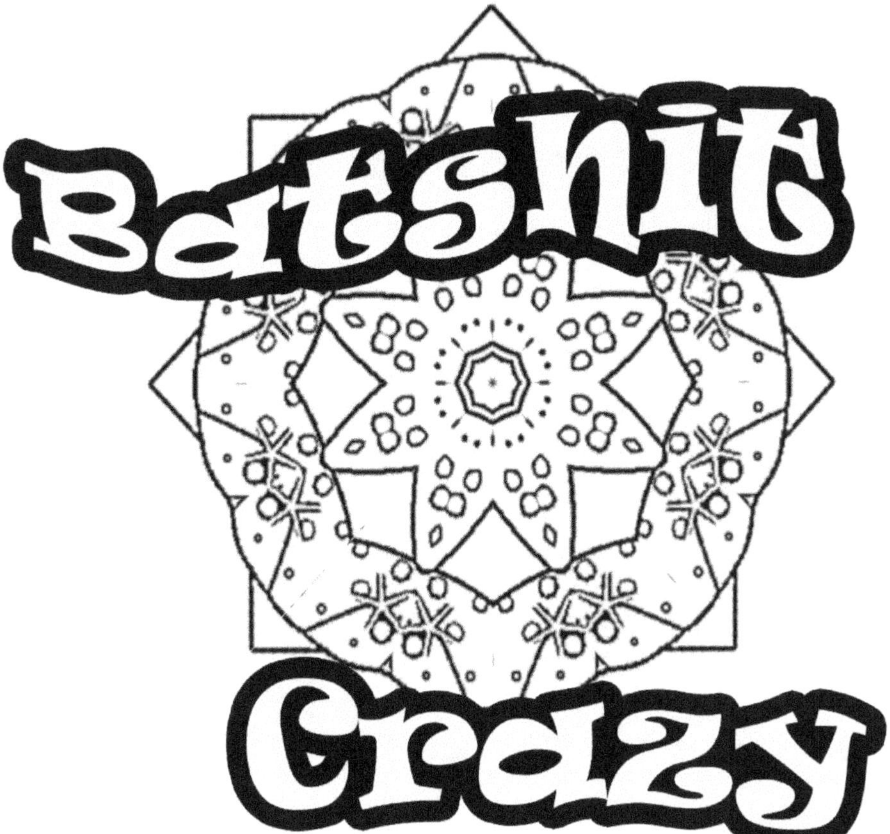
Batshit
Crazy

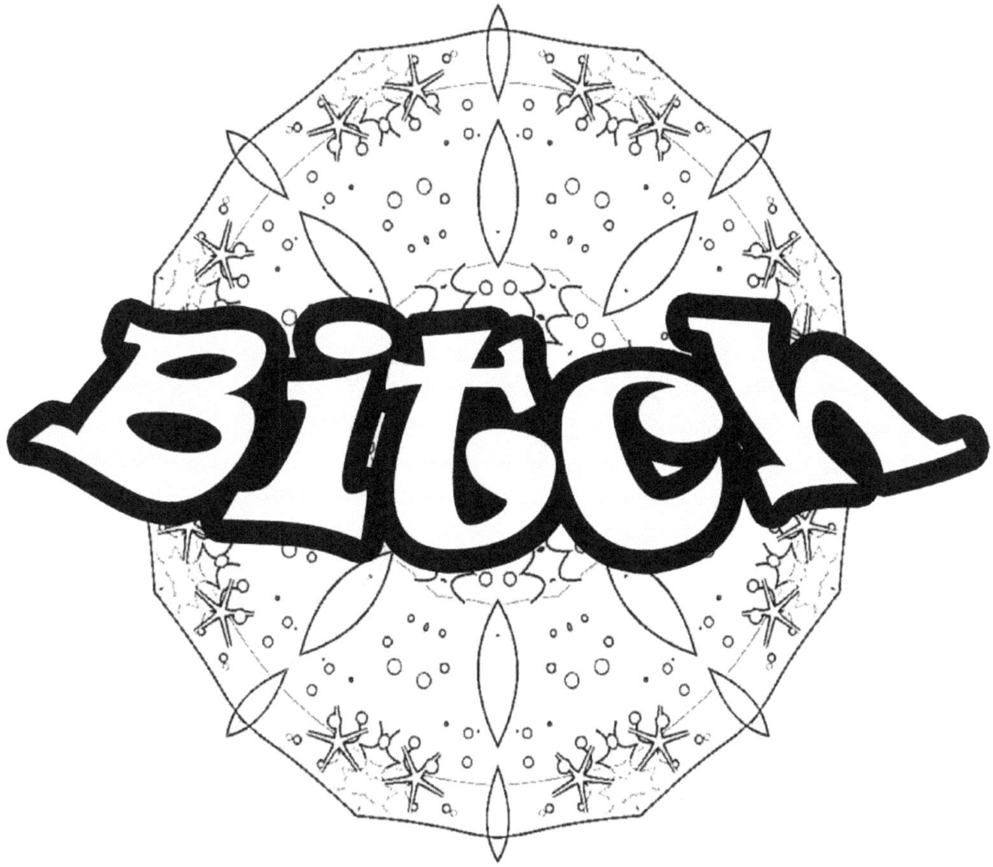
Bitch

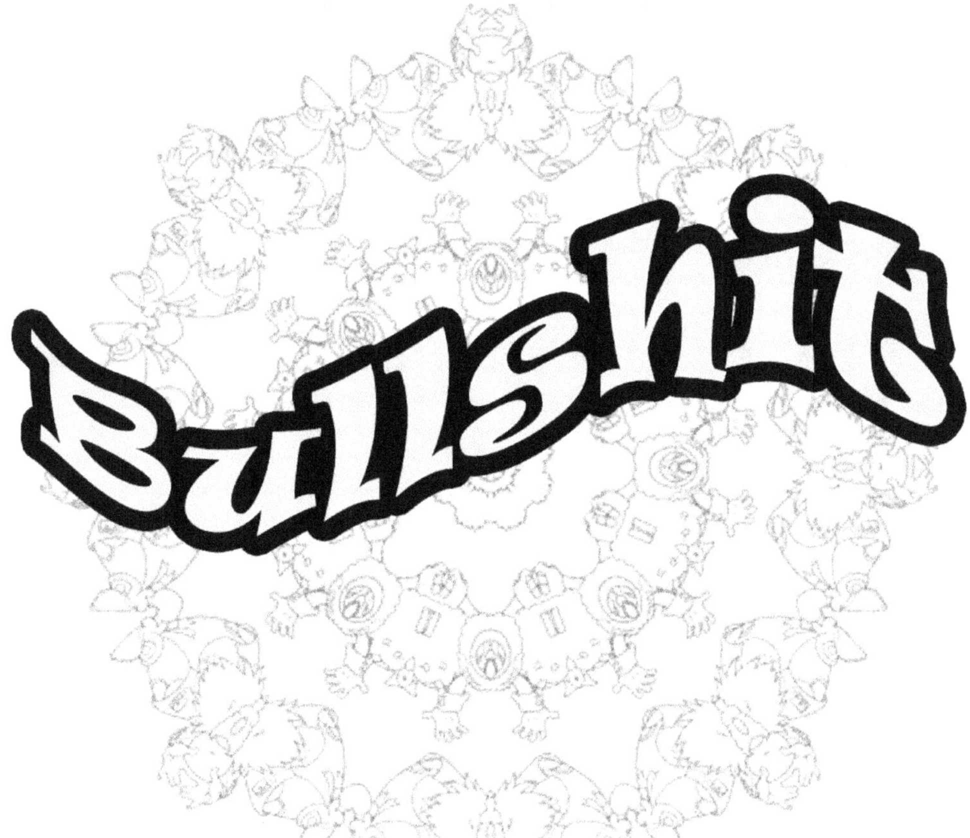
Bullshit

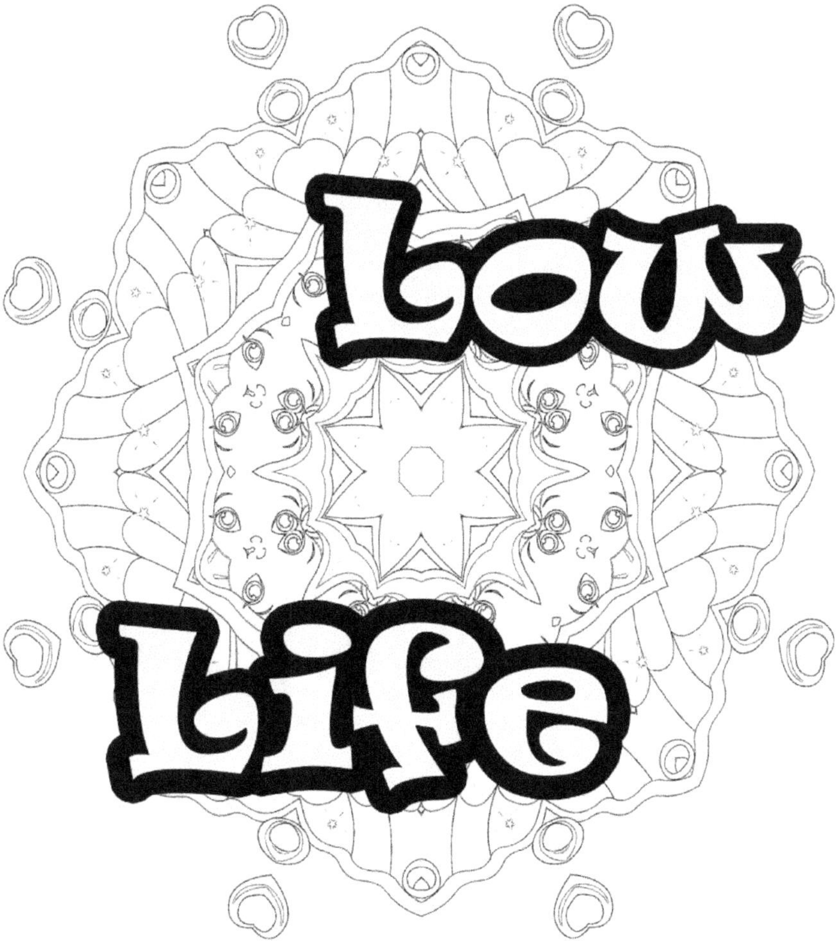
Low
Life

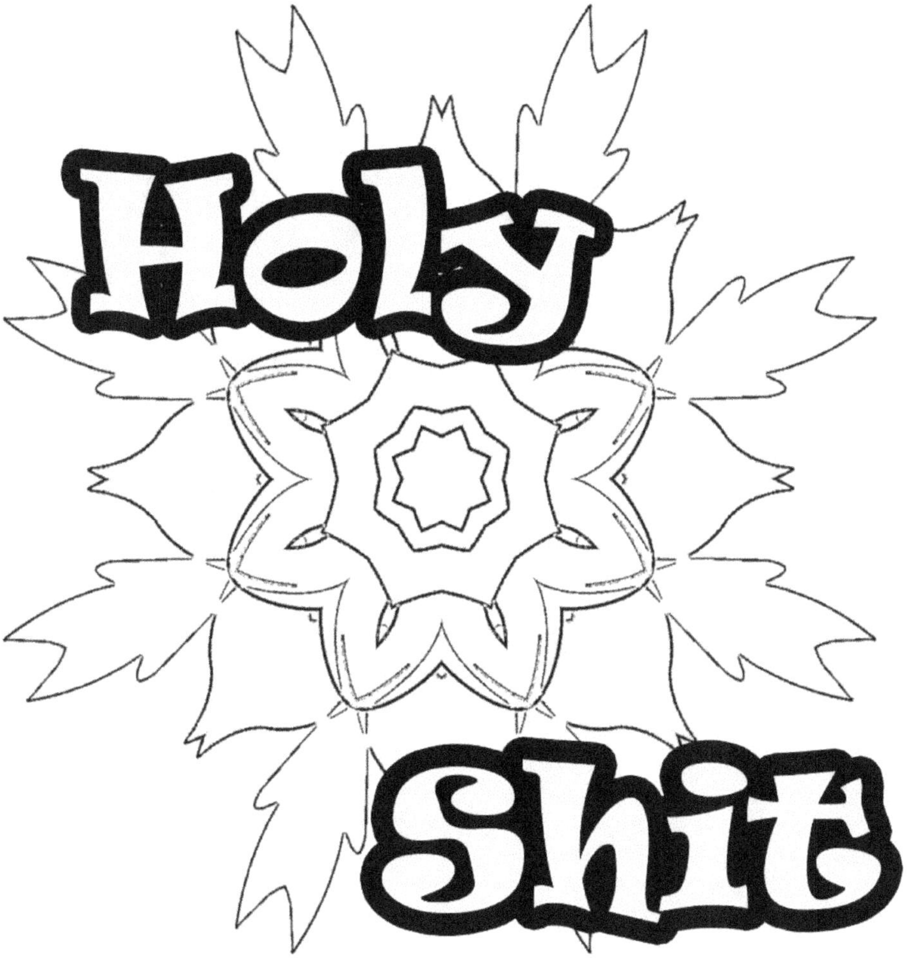
Holy
Shit

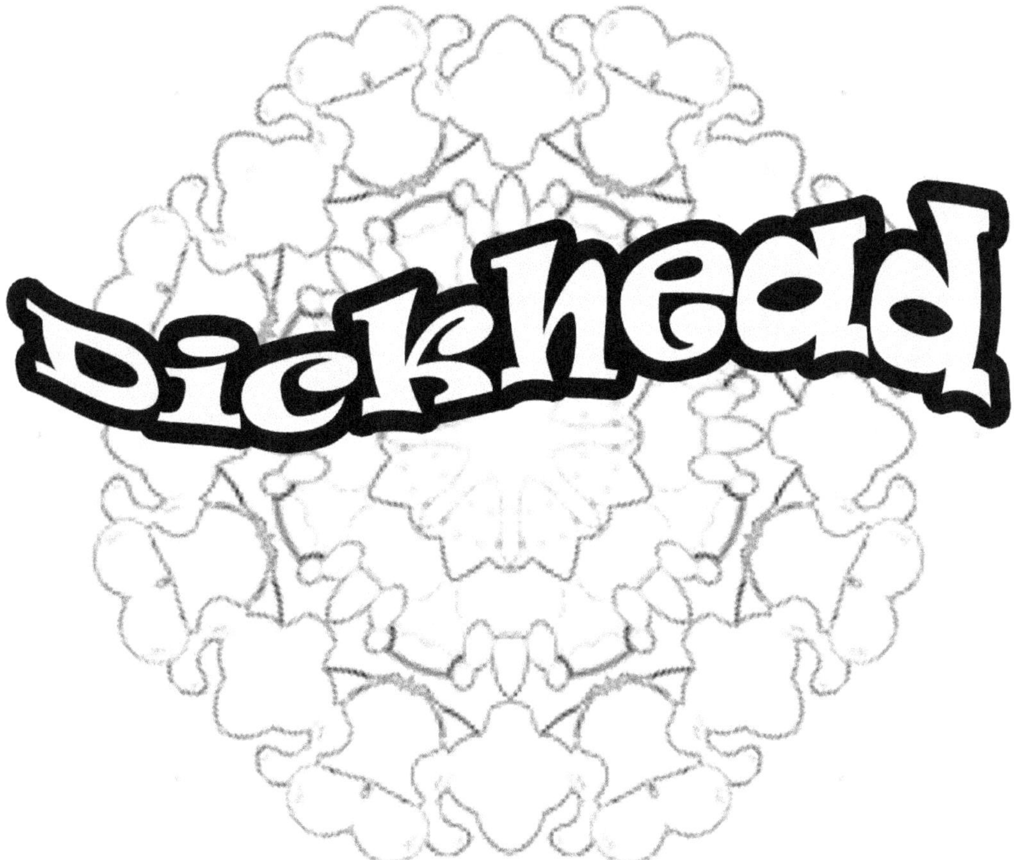
Dickhead

Zero

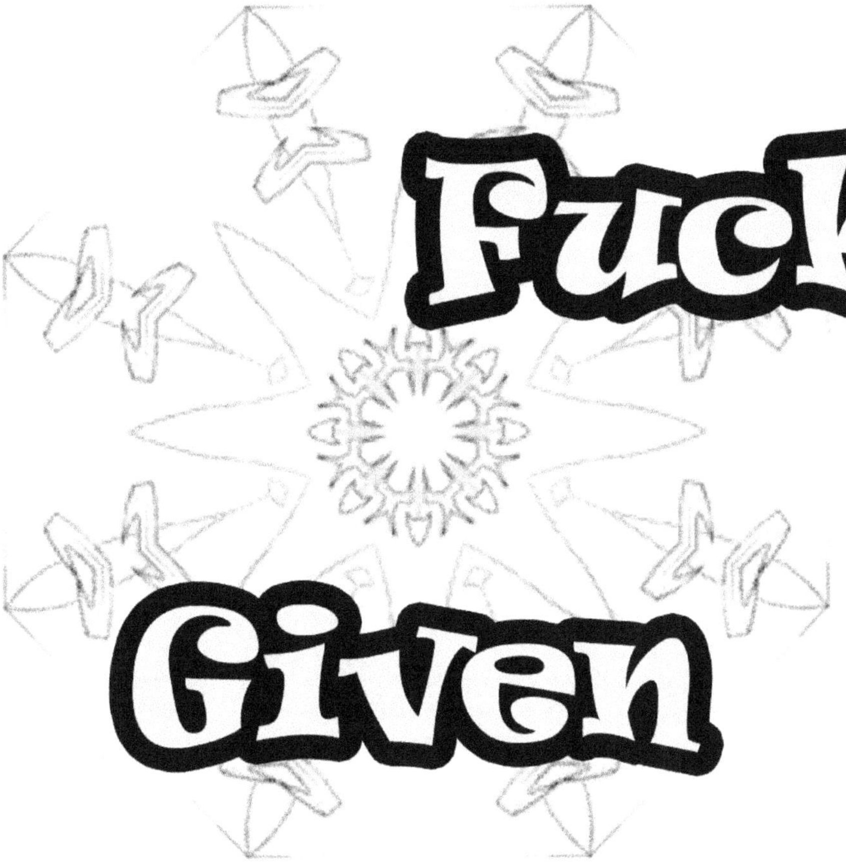

Fuck

Given

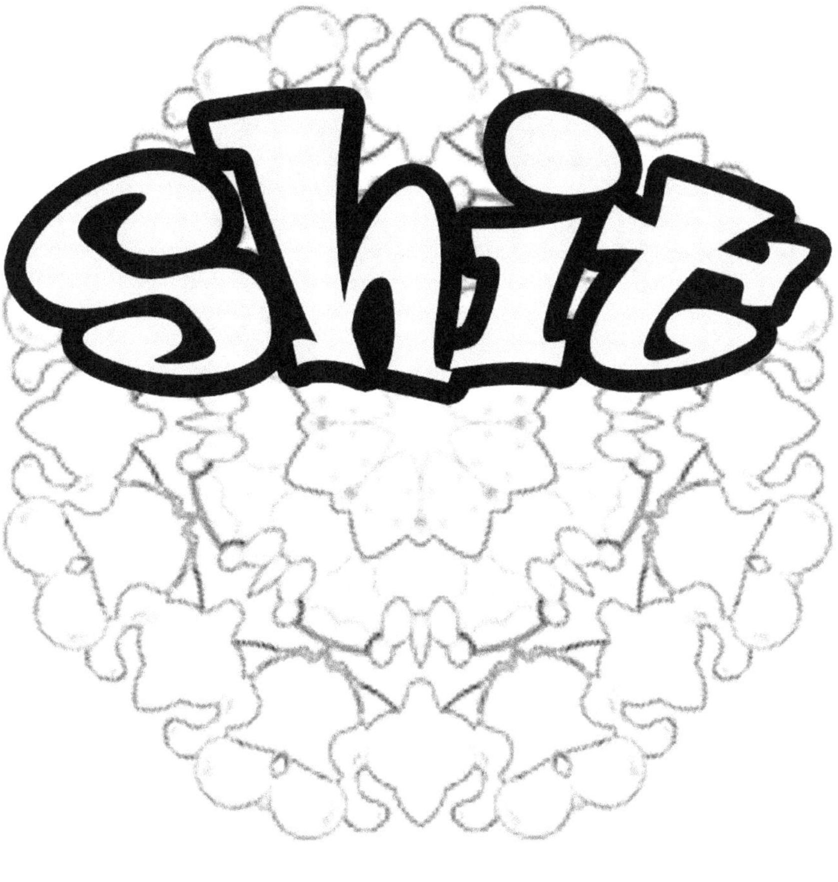
shit

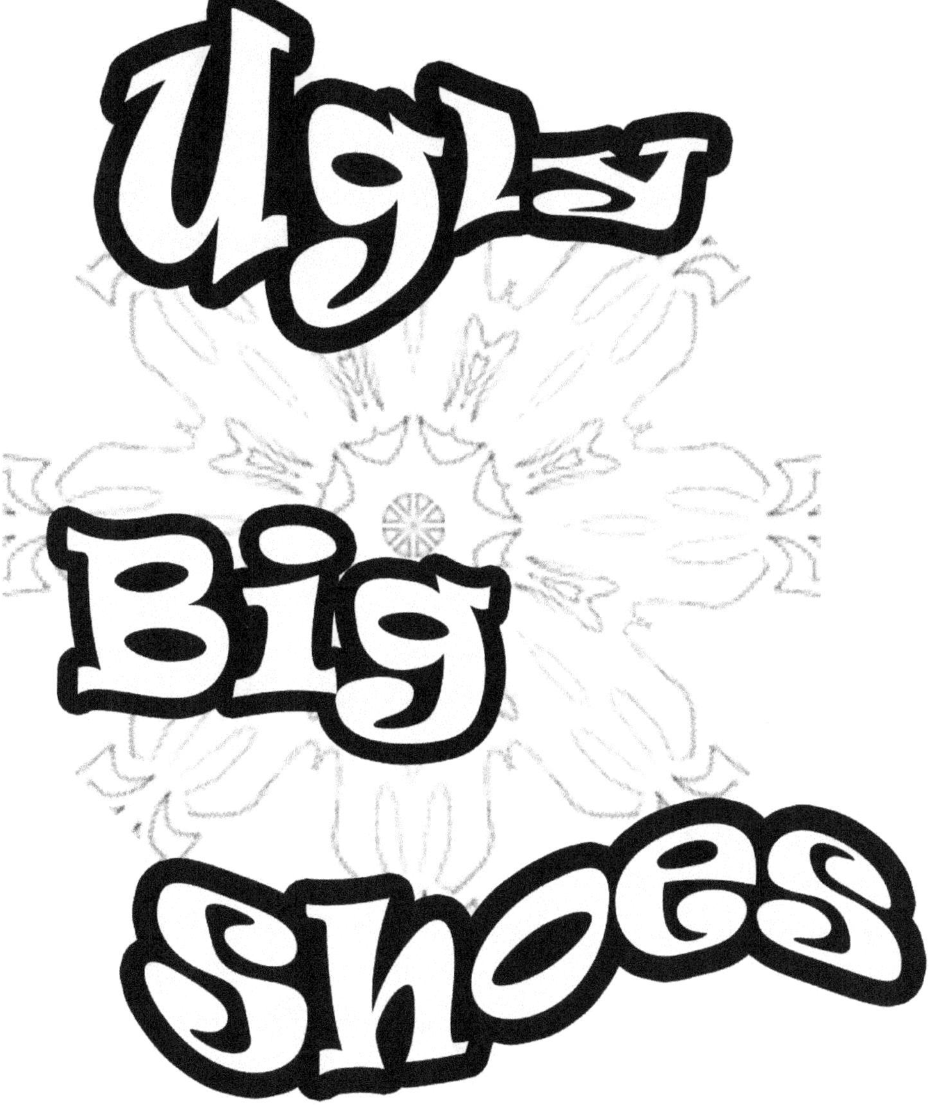
Ugly
Big
Shoes

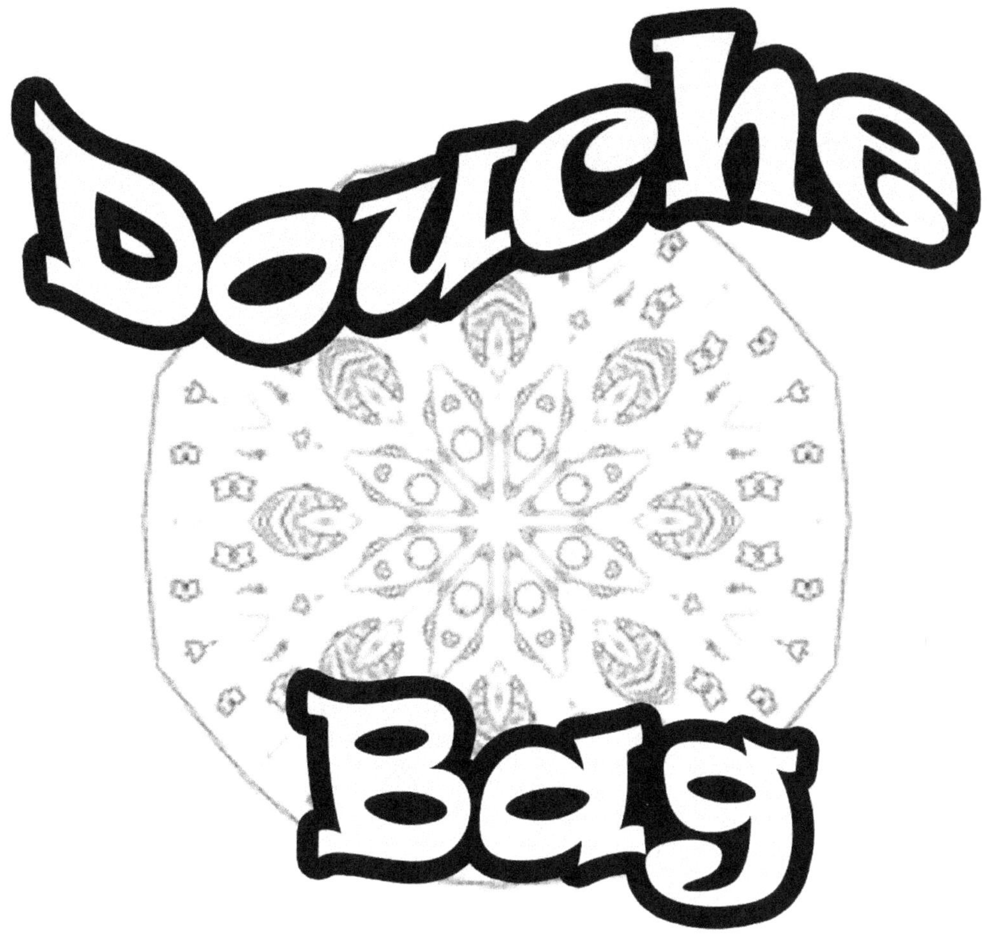
Douche
Bag

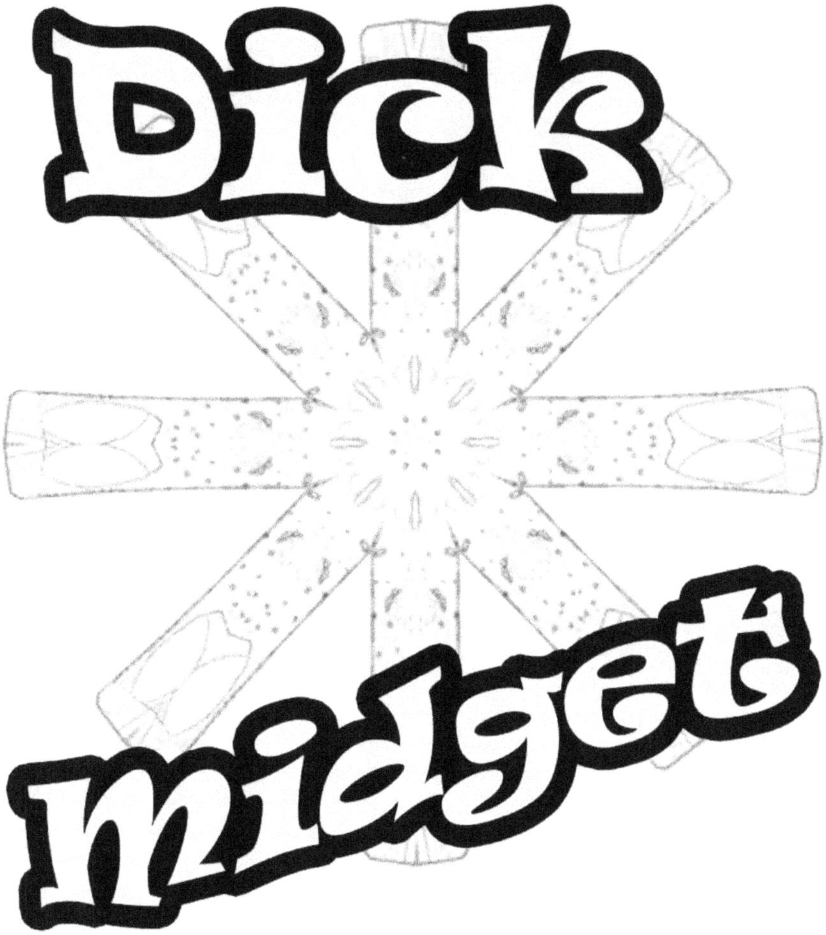
Dick
midget

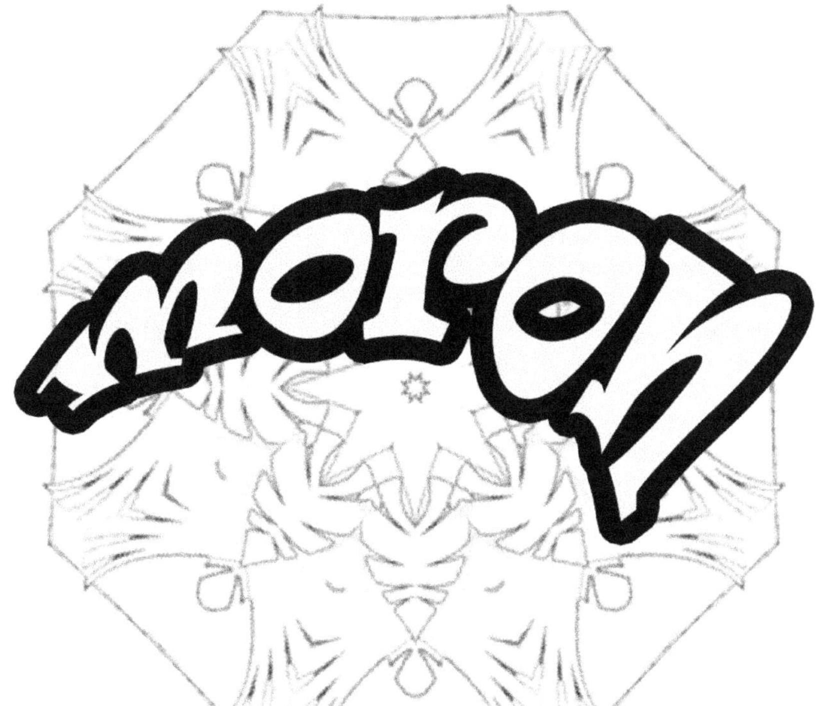
moron

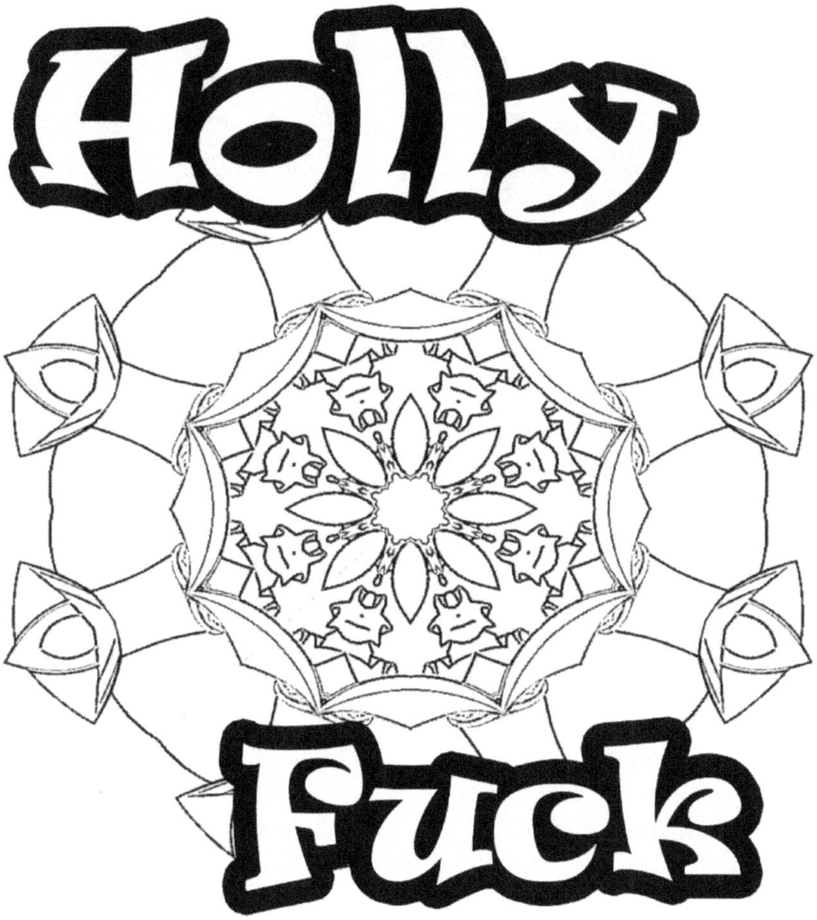
Holly
Fuck

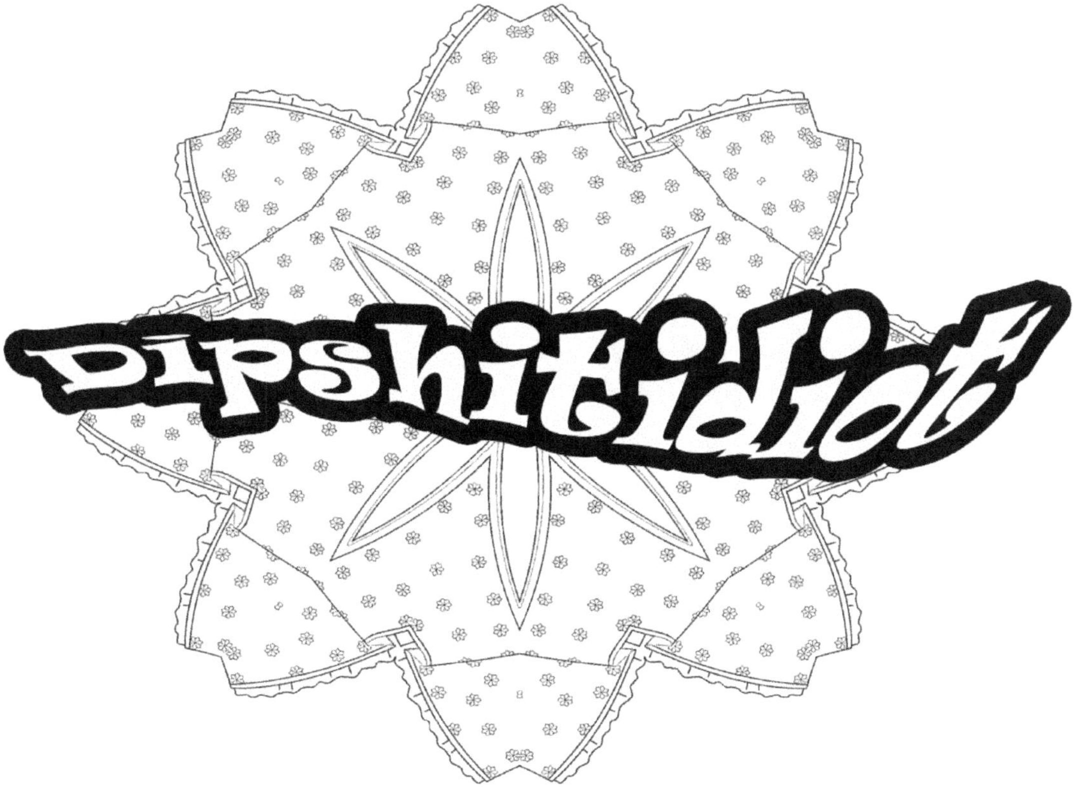
Dipshitidiot

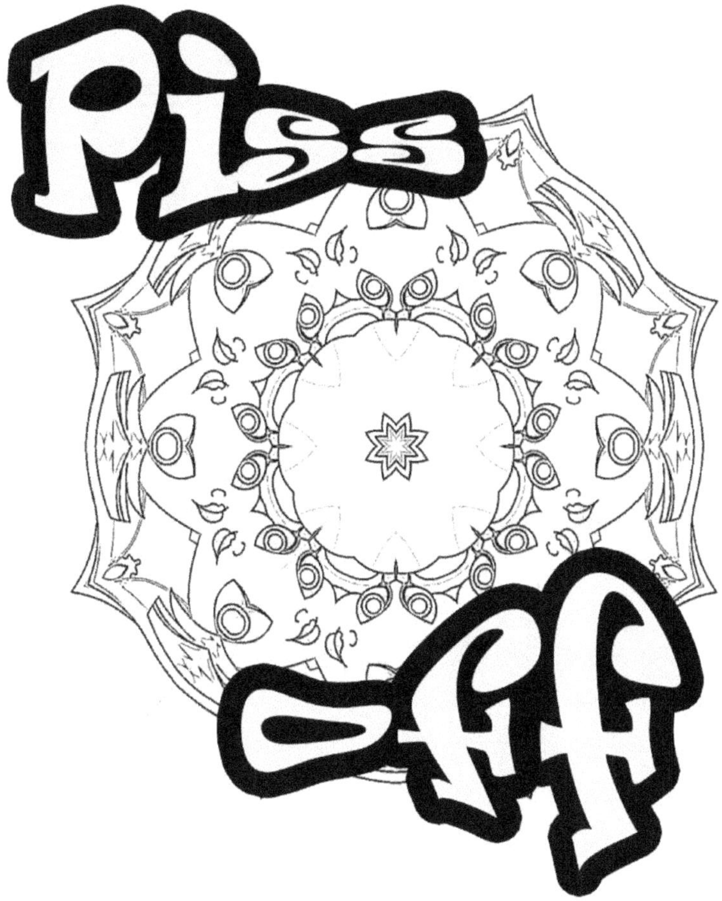
Piss
off

www.ingramcontent.com/pod-product-compliance
Lightning Source LLC
Chambersburg PA
CBHW080642190526
45169CB00009B/3468
* 9 7 8 1 5 3 2 8 1 6 8 1 9 *